SPACE DISCOVERY GUIDES

PLUTO

A SPACE DISCOVERY GUIDE

James Roland

Lerner Publications ◆ Minneapolis

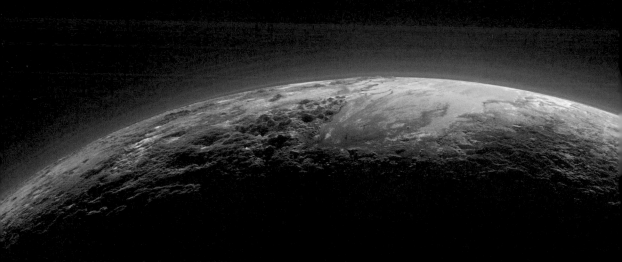

Lerner Publications Company
A division of Lerner Publishing Group, Inc.
241 First Avenue North
Minneapolis, MN 55401 USA

For reading levels and more information, look up this title at
www.lernerbooks.com.

Main body text set in Avenir LT Std 65 Medium 11.5/17.5.
Typeface provided by Adobe Systems.

Library of Congress Cataloging-in-Publication Data

Names: Roland, James, author.
Title: Pluto : a space discovery guide / James Roland.
Description: Minneapolis : Lerner Publications, [2017] | Series: Space discovery
    guides | Audience: Ages 9–12. | Audience: Grades 4 to 6. | Includes
    bibliographical references and index.
Identifiers: LCCN 2016018637 (print) | LCCN 2016023001 (ebook) | ISBN
    9781512425871 (lb : alk. paper) | ISBN 9781512427967 (eb pdf)
Subjects: LCSH: New Horizons (Spacecraft)—Juvenile literature. | Pluto (Dwarf
    planet)—Juvenile literature. | Kuiper Belt—Juvenile literature.
Classification: LCC QB701 .R65 2017 (print) | LCC QB701 (ebook) | DDC
    523.49/22—dc23

LC record available at https://lccn.loc.gov/2016018637

Manufactured in the United States of America
1-41355-23299-6/17/2016

TABLE OF CONTENTS

INTRODUCTION
MYSTERY SOLVED

An image of Pluto taken by *New Horizons* shows icy mountains and flat plains.

Nine and a half years after it blasted off from Florida's east coast, the National Aeronautics and Space Administration's (NASA) *New Horizons* spacecraft sent back the first-ever close-up images of Pluto. The images showed icy mountains and carved-up plains. Scientists learned about Pluto's atmosphere, its weather, and its moons. They discovered that Pluto may have lakes and rivers of liquid nitrogen. There may even be volcanoes that erupt with frozen nitrogen.

Pluto has been a mystery to astronomers for years. Because it is so far away, much of what scientists knew about Pluto's size, orbits, and surface came from theories. For years, scientists

An artist's rendering shows *New Horizons* approaching Pluto.

thought that Pluto was probably an icy rock covered in craters. But scientists at NASA wanted to know for sure about Pluto's atmosphere, moons, and surroundings. They wanted to finally explore this tiny world near the end of the solar system.

The search for answers began with a roar of smoke and fire on a launchpad at Cape Canaveral Air Force Station in Florida on January 19, 2006. On that sunny afternoon, a massive rocket blasted off carrying *New Horizons*. The spacecraft embarked on

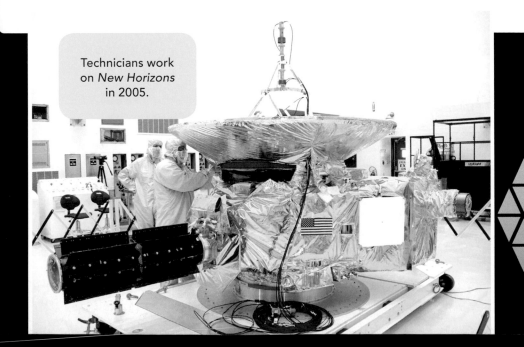

Technicians work on *New Horizons* in 2005.

a journey of more than 3 billion miles (4.8 billion kilometers) to reach Pluto and take pictures of the dwarf planet. This was the longest mission to a planet in the history of space travel. *New Horizons* zoomed away from Earth at more than 36,000 miles (58,000 km) per hour, making it one of the fastest spacecraft in history.

New Horizons launches from Cape Canaveral Air Force Station aboard an Atlas V rocket in 2006.

Before the *New Horizons* launch, mission lead scientist Alan Stern said the mission would be the crowning achievement of NASA's exploration of the solar system. It would also be one of the most ambitious. "It takes us 4 billion miles [6 billion km] away and 4 billion years back in time," he said.

When *New Horizons* finally reached Pluto in July 2015, the pictures it sent back stunned astronomers. The information made scientists rethink much of what they had once thought about the former planet. But the new information was also fascinating and exciting.

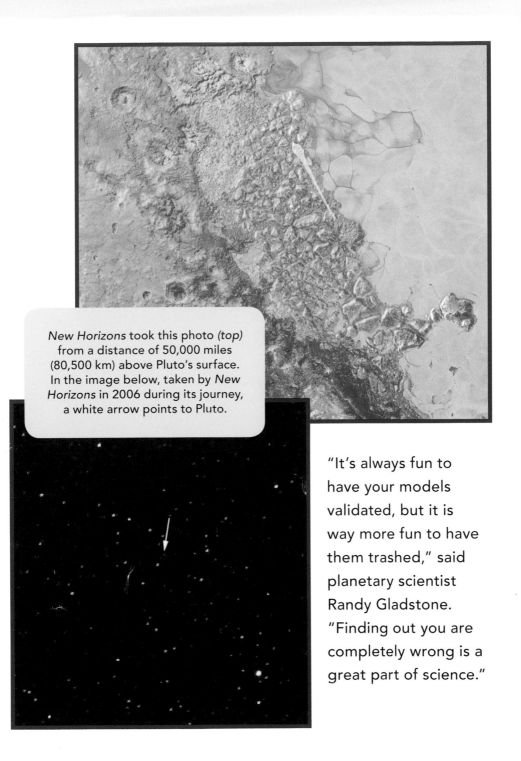

New Horizons took this photo *(top)* from a distance of 50,000 miles (80,500 km) above Pluto's surface. In the image below, taken by *New Horizons* in 2006 during its journey, a white arrow points to Pluto.

"It's always fun to have your models validated, but it is way more fun to have them trashed," said planetary scientist Randy Gladstone. "Finding out you are completely wrong is a great part of science."

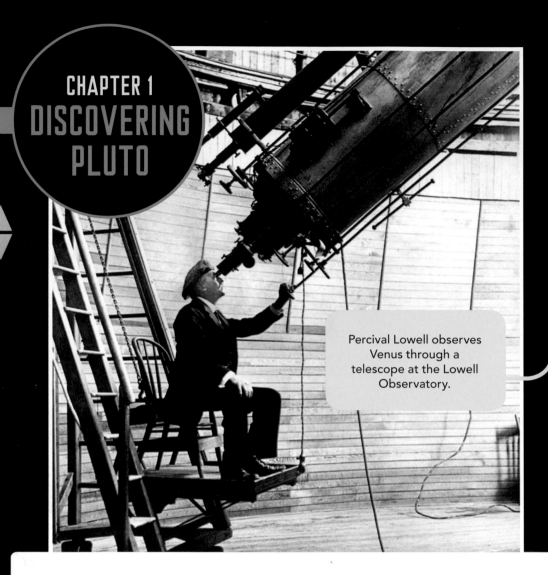

CHAPTER 1
DISCOVERING PLUTO

Percival Lowell observes Venus through a telescope at the Lowell Observatory.

Shortly after the planet Neptune was discovered in 1846, astronomers began debating whether there might be a ninth planet farther out in the solar system. There seemed to be something other than Neptune affecting the orbit of Uranus. One of the big believers in a ninth planet was a rich Bostonian named Percival Lowell. He was an avid astronomer who built an observatory in Flagstaff, Arizona, in 1894. He began searching for the ninth planet from his observatory in 1906.

This building is part of the Lowell Observatory in Arizona.

Lowell and a team of astronomers searched the skies for "Planet X" from their base at the Lowell Observatory. With a telescope, they took pictures of the sky every night. Lowell never found the planet, but he searched until his death in 1916.

In the late 1920s, a special photographic telescope known as an astrograph was built at the Lowell Observatory to search again for

This telescope at the Lowell Observatory was used to discover Pluto.

Planet X. In 1929 Clyde Tombaugh, a young assistant astronomer with no formal training, was hired at the Lowell Observatory to join the search for the ninth planet. Tombaugh spent the next ten months taking pictures of the sky.

Tombaugh made a series of special photographs of the region of space suspected to have the elusive planet.

Clyde Tombaugh poses with the telescope he used to discover Pluto *(above)*. Tombaugh used this blink comparator to study the sky and find Pluto *(right)*.

DISCOVERY OF THE PLANET PLUTO

January 23, 1930

January 29, 1930

The white arrows point to Pluto in two images taken by Tombaugh.

He made images of the stars and space in this region on glass sheets called photographic plates. Then he used a machine called a blink comparator to compare his images. The machine could place images on top of one another and go back and forth quickly between them. Stars would be in the same place in photos taken days apart, but an orbiting planet would move.

On February 18, 1930, Tombaugh noticed that a speck from images taken a month earlier appeared to move. It was in one place on one plate and in a different spot on another plate. Tombaugh had discovered what would be considered the solar system's ninth planet. It was known as Planet X. The discovery was officially announced on March 13, 1930. It would have been Lowell's birthday.

NAMING THE NEW PLANET

News of Tombaugh's discovery spread quickly around the world. In England an elderly man named Falconer Madan read a newspaper story about the new planet to his daughter and eleven-year-old granddaughter over breakfast on March 14, 1930. Madan's granddaughter, Venetia Burney, knew that the other planets were named for mythological gods and goddesses. She suggested the name Pluto, the Roman god of the underworld.

Venetia Burney suggested the name Pluto for the ninth planet.

Madan, who had been head of the Bodleian Library at the University of Oxford, loved the idea. He told Herbert Hall Turner, a friend who had been an astronomy professor at Oxford. Turner contacted the astronomers at Lowell. They liked Venetia's idea, especially because of the first two letters in Pluto. They are the same as Percival Lowell's initials. In May 1930, Pluto was officially named.

PLUTO: AN ICY DWARF?

Pluto's vast distance from Earth meant that astronomers learned little about the planet for many years. Astronomers determined its orbit around the sun. They came up with theories about the

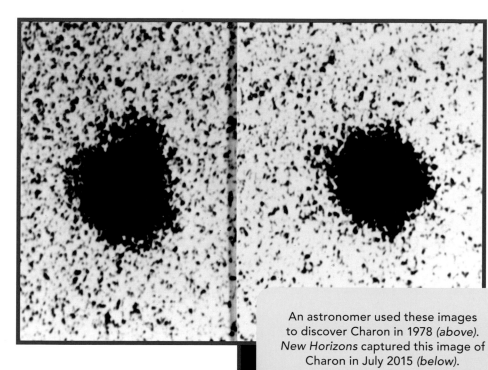

An astronomer used these images to discover Charon in 1978 *(above)*. *New Horizons* captured this image of Charon in July 2015 *(below)*.

gases in its atmosphere and the minerals on its surface. In 1978 a large moon was discovered orbiting Pluto. The moon was named Charon, another character from ancient Roman mythology.

In 2003 astronomers made a discovery that would completely change the way they thought about Pluto. In a region of space beyond Neptune known as the Kuiper Belt, they found another round, planetlike object. The object, named Eris, was similar to Pluto. And scientists discovered that the Kuiper Belt was filled with other small planetlike objects too. Scientists realized that the solar system might have dozens or even hundreds of these small planets past Neptune. So the International Astronomical Union (IAU)—a group of astronomers that has been classifying planets and other objects in space for more than one hundred years—voted to place Pluto in a separate category from rocky planets like Earth and Mars and big gas giants like Saturn. Pluto would no longer be considered the ninth planet in the solar system. Instead, Pluto, along with Eris and another small planet called Ceres, would be known as a dwarf planet, or an icy dwarf.

An artist's impression shows what Eris may look like. The dwarf planet is thought to be about the size of Pluto and have a very reflective surface covered in frost.

This artist's image shows Ceres in the asteroid belt beyond the orbit of Mars *(above)*. A NASA spacecraft captured this image of Ceres in 2015 *(inset)*.

▶ SUPPORT FOR PLUTO

The reclassification of Pluto was seen as a demotion by a lot of people who liked the solar system's smallest, most mysterious planet. Students around the world wrote letters to the IAU. They were joined in their protest by plenty of adults too. Some people are still trying to get the IAU to reconsider its decision.

But Mike Brown, a California Institute of Technology planetary scientist who discovered Eris, said it wouldn't make sense to

call all the planetlike objects in the solar system planets. Dwarf planets behave differently from the other planets. The eight official planets have orbits around the sun that are clear of other objects. Pluto and other dwarf planets orbit amid asteroids and other objects in the Kuiper Belt.

Planetary scientist Scott Sheppard of the Carnegie Institution for Science in Washington, DC, said that Pluto's history shows why science is so exciting. "This debate shows people, especially kids, that science is always evolving, and it's exciting," Sheppard said. "You should get involved in science, because there's a lot more to learn out there."

And as scientists began receiving photos from *New Horizons*, Sheppard's statement was proven true. It's not just Pluto's history that's exciting. Its present is pretty incredible as well.

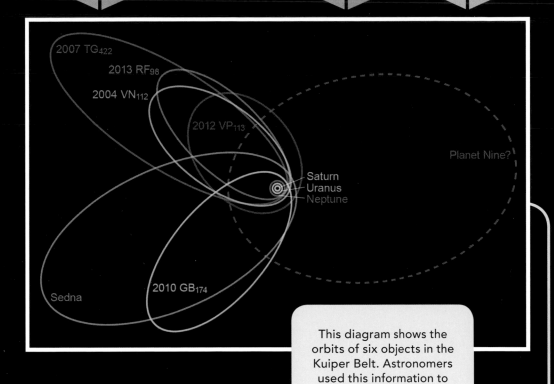

2007 TG$_{422}$

2013 RF$_{98}$

2004 VN$_{112}$

2012 VP$_{113}$

Saturn
Uranus
Neptune

Planet Nine?

Sedna

2010 GB$_{174}$

This diagram shows the orbits of six objects in the Kuiper Belt. Astronomers used this information to predict the presence of a ninth planet.

A New Planet X

In January 2016, astronomers announced that a new Planet X may exist in a distant region of space. These astronomers have found six objects in the Kuiper Belt that are all tilted at the same angle. This angle is different from the way Earth and the other seven planets of the solar system are tilted.

The odds of these objects all randomly tilting the same way are 0.007 percent. So astronomers suggest that the gravitational pull of a large planet far past Neptune may be causing those six objects to tilt in the same way. Scientists predict that this planet may be ten times as massive as Earth and its orbit may be twenty times farther from the sun than Neptune. So it would take this planet between ten thousand and twenty thousand years to orbit the sun. Astronomers haven't seen the planet yet, but the search is on again for a ninth planet.

An artist's image shows an object in the Kuiper Belt 4 billion miles (6 billion km) from the sun.

The solar system is broken up into three zones that contain three kinds of planets. The first zone consists of rocky planets, the second contains the gas giant planets, and the third is the Kuiper Belt, where Pluto and other icy dwarfs are. There are more of these icy dwarfs than any other kind of planet. Before *New Horizons*, the United States had sent space probes to visit all eight planets in the solar system. But no spacecraft had ever explored a dwarf planet.

In 2002 a report by the National Research Council said that without exploring the third zone of the solar system or any icy dwarfs, knowledge of the solar system was incomplete. The report by leading US scientists and engineers ranked the exploration of Pluto and the Kuiper Belt as the highest priority for planetary science. It said that this region was the gateway to the rest of the galaxy. In 2003 NASA authorized the *New Horizons* mission.

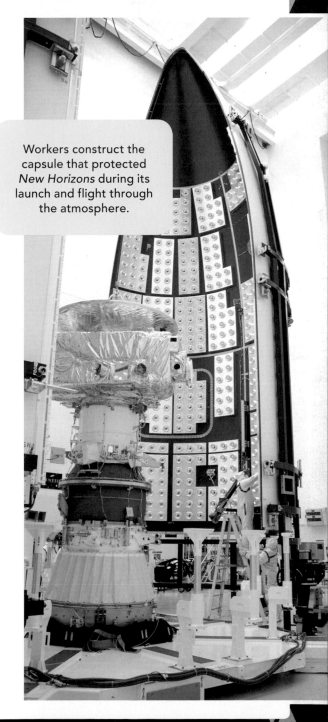

Workers construct the capsule that protected *New Horizons* during its launch and flight through the atmosphere.

A TEN-YEAR TRIP

Thousands of engineers and scientists worked for more than two years to make sure the *New Horizons* mission would succeed. The Atlas V rocket, with *New Horizons* firmly attached on top, was moved to the launchpad at

New Horizons is prepared for liftoff in Cape Canaveral.

Cape Canaveral on January 17, 2006. But strong winds swirled off the Atlantic Ocean for two days. No one wanted to risk New Horizons. The weather had to be perfect. Finally, on January 19, 2006, at 2 p.m., the wind calmed, the sun shone, and New Horizons left Earth for the far end of the solar system.

After launch, New Horizons received an additional boost from Earth's orbit, and the spacecraft roared through space at about 100,000 miles (160,900 km) per hour. But when it neared Jupiter a little more than a year later, New Horizons had slowed to about 43,000 miles (69,200 km) per hour.

The astronomers controlling New Horizons planned to use Jupiter to give the spacecraft a boost known as a gravity assist. Because of the gravitational pull of Jupiter, New Horizons picked up speed as it moved toward the planet. Jupiter's motion added energy to New Horizons. It sped away from Jupiter at more than 52,000 miles (83,700 km) per hour.

This photo, composed of multiple images taken by *New Horizons* during it's Jupiter flyby in early 2007, shows Jupiter and one of its moons.

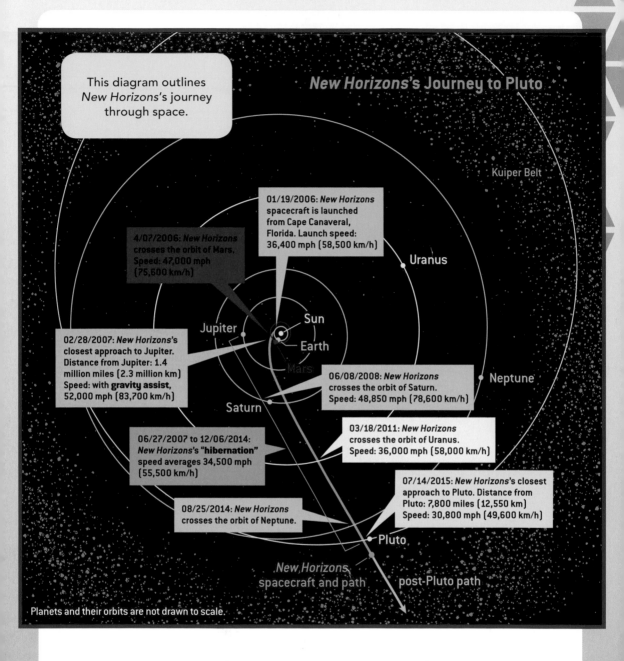

This diagram outlines *New Horizons*'s journey through space.

New Horizons's Journey to Pluto

Kuiper Belt

01/19/2006: *New Horizons* spacecraft is launched from Cape Canaveral, Florida. Launch speed: 36,400 mph (58,500 km/h)

4/07/2006: *New Horizons* crosses the orbit of Mars. Speed: 47,000 mph (75,600 km/h)

02/28/2007: *New Horizons*'s closest approach to Jupiter. Distance from Jupiter: 1.4 million miles (2.3 million km) Speed: with **gravity assist**, 52,000 mph (83,700 km/h)

06/08/2008: *New Horizons* crosses the orbit of Saturn. Speed: 48,850 mph (78,600 km/h)

03/18/2011: *New Horizons* crosses the orbit of Uranus. Speed: 36,000 mph (58,000 km/h)

06/27/2007 to 12/06/2014: *New Horizons*'s "**hibernation**" speed averages 34,500 mph (55,500 km/h)

07/14/2015: *New Horizons*'s closest approach to Pluto. Distance from Pluto: 7,800 miles (12,550 km) Speed: 30,800 mph (49,600 km/h)

08/25/2014: *New Horizons* crosses the orbit of Neptune.

Uranus

Jupiter

Sun

Earth

Mars

Saturn

Neptune

Pluto

New Horizons spacecraft and path

post-Pluto path

Planets and their orbits are not drawn to scale.

Between 2007 and 2014, *New Horizons* was in hibernation mode. It used only enough power to navigate and keep its other essential operations working. In 2014 *New Horizons* woke up to get ready for its 2015 flyby of Pluto.

NEW HORIZONS

To reach Pluto and be able to relay photographs back to Earth, the *New Horizons* spacecraft had to have specific equipment and be built in a certain way. The triangular spacecraft is a little bigger than a minivan and weighs 1,054 pounds (478 kilograms). It has a large, round antenna on one side. Most of the communication with Earth uses this antenna. *New Horizons* also has digital recorders that store information in its onboard memory. Along with pictures, *New Horizons* gathered information about the gases on and near Pluto and measured Pluto's temperature.

Some spacecraft and satellites can use solar energy to keep working. The Hubble Space Telescope, which orbits Earth, has large solar panels to collect the sun's energy. This energy fuels Hubble. But Pluto is so far from the sun that solar power couldn't provide the spacecraft with enough energy to keep going. Instead, *New Horizons* is powered by a radioisotope

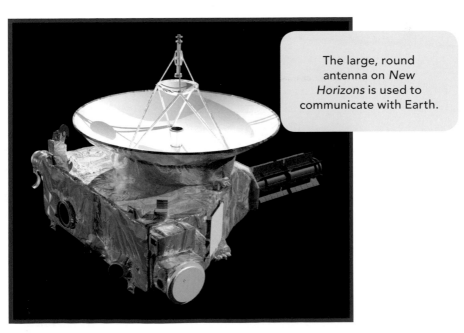

The large, round antenna on *New Horizons* is used to communicate with Earth.

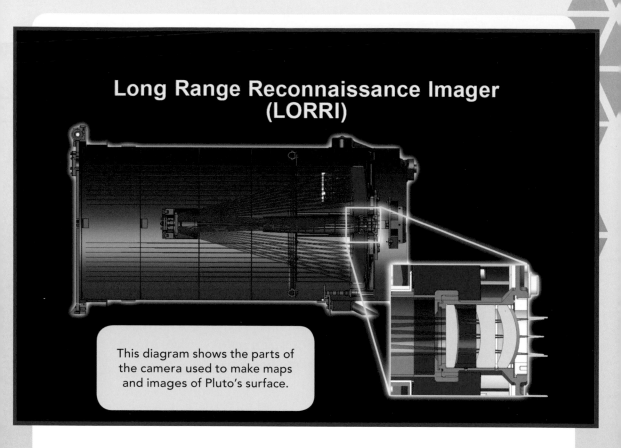

Long Range Reconnaissance Imager (LORRI)

This diagram shows the parts of the camera used to make maps and images of Pluto's surface.

thermoelectric generator. This device uses a type of plutonium that gives off heat as it decays. This means *New Horizons* is nuclear-powered.

The device most responsible for capturing images of Pluto is called the Long Range Reconnaissance Imager (LORRI). This telescopic camera created maps and recorded detailed information about Pluto's surface and terrain.

▶ GUIDING *NEW HORIZONS*

A team of scientists and engineers working at the Applied Physics Laboratory steers *New Horizons* and directs its cameras and satellites from Earth. Alice Bowman, the first woman to be a mission operations manager at APL, is in charge of operations. One of her jobs is to read every line of computer code that is sent to *New Horizons*. All the instructions for navigation, sending images and other data to Earth, and any other operations are sent in coded language through radio signals. "I'm the last one who signs off on everything we send to the spacecraft," Bowman explained. "I want to make sure it's perfect."

Because *New Horizons* is so far away from Earth, the radio signals between Earth and the spacecraft are pretty weak when they arrive. And it takes about four and a half hours for signals to travel between *New Horizons* and the APL. On Earth huge antennae in Australia, Spain, and California make up the Deep

Alice Bowman attends a press conference after *New Horizons* completed its flyby of Pluto.

The Canberra Deep Space Communication Complex in Australia is one of three complexes that make up the Deep Space Network (above). This 230-foot (70-meter) antenna in Australia is used to communicate with New Horizons (left).

Space Network. Only three of the antennae are large enough to communicate with *New Horizons*. These antennae are 230 feet (70 m) across. They exchange signals with *New Horizons*, but they also communicate with other spacecraft and satellites. So *New Horizons* has to wait its turn to get in touch with Earth.

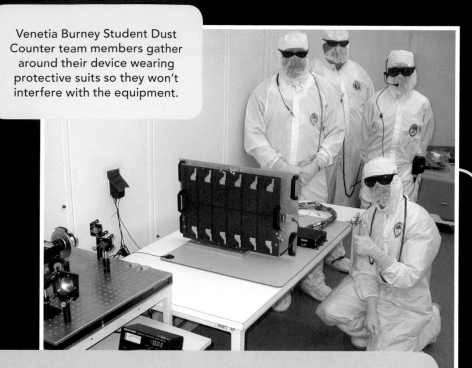

Venetia Burney Student Dust Counter team members gather around their device wearing protective suits so they won't interfere with the equipment.

Counting Dust

Most of the design and construction of *New Horizons* was planned and executed by NASA and Johns Hopkins University Applied Physics Laboratory (APL) in Maryland. But one feature on the spacecraft was designed and built by students from the University of Colorado. It's called the Venetia Burney Student Dust Counter (SDC), in honor of the girl who named Pluto in 1930. The SDC analyzes dust that strikes *New Horizons* and sends that information back to Earth. Students and scientists believe that the elements that make up the dust will tell us about the materials that formed the planets, moons, and other objects in the solar system billions of years ago. This data may also help scientists understand more about the formation of planets in other star systems.

New Horizons digitally stores the photos it takes of Pluto. Each file is about 2.5 megabits. Because communications are slow and the files are large, scientists usually only receive about eleven LORRI images each day. Scientists planned for *New Horizons* to reach Pluto in July 2015, but they knew they wouldn't receive all the data from the spacecraft until more than a year later.

MISSING SPACECRAFT

Everything went according to plan until about ten days before *New Horizons* was to fly within 8,000 miles (12,875 km) of Pluto's surface. On July 4, 2015, the operations team lost contact with the spacecraft. Lead scientist Stern and others stayed through the

Several people work with *New Horizons* at the mission operation center at the APL.

An artist's rendering of *New Horizons* flying through space

night to try to regain contact. Hundreds of commands were sent to *New Horizons* to try to reset the spacecraft's main computer and reestablish communication.

"It's a people story," Stern said later of the efforts to find *New Horizons*. "People literally sleeping on the floor, staying all night, night after night. People buckled down and were totally committed to the spacecraft's recovery."

After about three days, contact was made again between Earth and *New Horizons*. And it was just in time. The flyby was a week away.

CHAPTER 3
PLUTO UP CLOSE

This image shows the bright, heart-shaped Tombaugh Regio with the dark area to the left.

As *New Horizons* approached Pluto, some of the earliest photos it sent back to Earth showed interesting features on the surface of the icy dwarf. A large, bright, heart-shaped area was next to a dark shape. Scientists began calling the heart-shaped region Tombaugh Regio, after the man who discovered Pluto. The dark area was nicknamed the whale. The heart and the whale were the first indications that the surface of Pluto might be more interesting than scientists originally thought.

As *New Horizons* finally made its flyby of Pluto on July 14, 2015, the spacecraft got as close as 7,800 miles (12,550 km) from the surface. While flying 30,800 miles (49,568 km) per hour, *New*

A crowd at the APL counts down to *New Horizons*'s closest approach to Pluto.

Horizons took and stored thousands of photos of Pluto and began slowly sending them to Earth. As *New Horizons* sent more and more photos to Earth, scientists learned fascinating and surprising things about the surface of Pluto. "*New Horizons* thrilled us during the July flyby with the first close images of Pluto, and as the spacecraft transmits the treasure trove of images in its onboard memory back to us, we continue to be amazed by what we see," said former astronaut John Grunsfeld.

MOUNTAINS AND PLAINS

Within Tombaugh Regio, scientists noticed what looked like mountains. They are about the size of the Rocky Mountains on Earth, sticking up 11,000 feet (3,350 m) from the surface of Pluto.

This *New Horizons* image shows a mountain range on the surface of Pluto.

Scientists knew that Pluto had a lot of nitrogen ice, but nitrogen ice is too soft to be able to form into a mountain. Instead, scientists think these mountains are made of water ice. Because temperatures are so cold on Pluto, water ice acts kind of like rock. It is hard enough to be able to form mountains.

Scientists were also surprised to find that while most of Pluto is covered in dents and craters, the region surrounding these mountains had no craters. This may mean the surface of Tombaugh Regio is relatively young—about one hundred million years old. According to Jeff Moore, a NASA researcher, "This is one of the youngest surfaces we've ever seen in the solar system." The region may even still be geologically active. The surface may be changing, smoothing out and filling in craters. If this is the case, scientists say they may have to rethink their understanding of how geology works on other planets. This geological activity may be caused by an unknown heat source within Pluto.

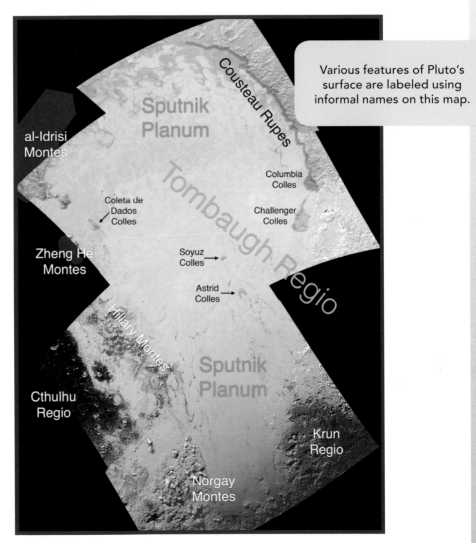

Various features of Pluto's surface are labeled using informal names on this map.

Along the edge of Tombaugh Regio, scientists also saw what they think may be volcanoes. A few mountains appear to have craters at their peaks. They look similar to how volcanoes on Earth look. Scientists are not sure that these mountains are volcanoes. But if they are, they may erupt with frozen nitrogen.

▶ SPUTNIK PLANUM

One of the most photographed parts of Pluto's surface is an area within the Tombaugh Regio called Sputnik Planum. This wide plain is named after *Sputnik 1*, the first man-made satellite to orbit Earth. Sputnik Planum has a smooth surface, but the surface is also broken into oddly shaped pieces. Scientists believe that the region is covered in glaciers made of nitrogen ice, carbon monoxide ice, and methane ice. At Pluto's temperature of −390°F (−234°C), these ices may be able to flow across the surface of Pluto. As these glaciers flow, they appear to carry broken pieces of water ice along with them. This water ice looks like floating hills across Sputnik Planum.

This image shows the icy surface of Sputnik Planum.

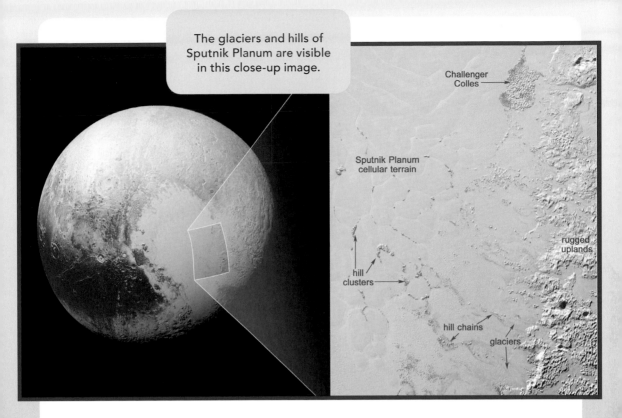

The glaciers and hills of Sputnik Planum are visible in this close-up image.

North of Sputnik Planum, scientists saw what looks like a frozen lake, probably made of nitrogen. Scientists believe there may be other lakes and rivers across Pluto. This flowing nitrogen may be what carved out the complex terrain of Pluto. And there may even be underground nitrogen rivers still flowing.

As scientists continue to collect and study photos and data, they are making more discoveries about Pluto. There is still a lot scientists don't know about how the surface of Pluto was formed and how it might continue to shift. But they are already developing theories about how the wind, weather, and atmosphere might act to create these complex mountains, glaciers, and volcanoes.

CHAPTER 4
BEYOND PLUTO

This *New Horizons* image shows the blue layers of Pluto's atmosphere.

As *New Horizons* flew past Pluto, it turned back to take a few more pictures. These images were lit by the sun, showing Pluto's incredible atmosphere in blue layers surrounding the dwarf planet. "Who would have expected a blue sky in the Kuiper Belt?" Stern asked. "It's glorious."

LAYERS OF BLUE

The photos of the layers of Pluto's atmosphere along with data collected by other instruments on *New Horizons* have shown scientists not only blue skies but also that the dwarf planet's atmosphere is much different than expected. The twenty layers of atmosphere extend at least 100 miles (161 km) above the surface of the icy dwarf. This is much higher than predicted. The atmosphere is made of nitrogen, methane, and carbon monoxide. Because gravity is not very strong on Pluto, scientists thought the gases would escape the atmosphere and be released into space. As *New Horizons* approached Pluto, it detected that nitrogen was leaving the icy dwarf. But scientists found that the atmosphere was not leaving as quickly as they had thought. And despite the leaking nitrogen, the atmosphere is still 98 percent nitrogen. So nitrogen may be entering the atmosphere from the surface of Pluto. And the cold temperatures of the highest layers of the atmosphere may keep the gases from escaping so quickly.

Scientists have said that the layers of Pluto's atmosphere may mean that the weather changes on Pluto each day, the same as on

A hazy sky surrounds Pluto.

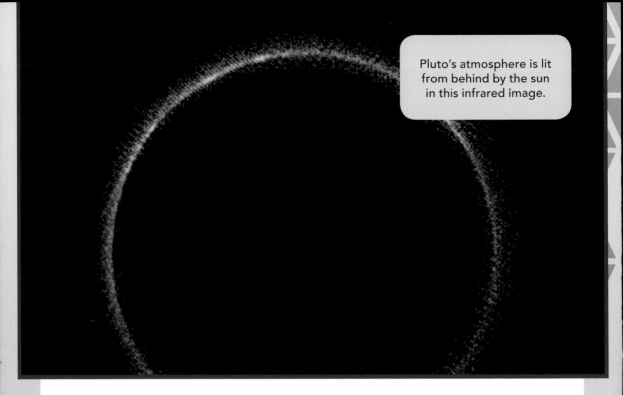

Pluto's atmosphere is lit from behind by the sun in this infrared image.

Earth. Pluto also has seasons. The dwarf planet is tilted and takes 248 years to orbit the sun. So for several years at a time, part of Pluto is dark and other parts see lots of sunlight. These seasons may have a lot to do with Pluto's terrain. Pluto's orbit also affects its atmosphere. When Pluto is closest to the sun, some of its ices thaw and enter the atmosphere. When Pluto is farther from the sun, the gases freeze to become ice once again.

PLUTO'S MANY MOONS

Along with learning about Pluto's surface, scientists working with *New Horizons* wanted to know about the moons orbiting the icy dwarf. Charon is Pluto's largest moon, at about half the size of the dwarf planet. But shortly before *New Horizons* was to take off, two more moons were discovered. They are called Nix and Hydra. And while *New Horizons* was flying toward Pluto, another two moons, Kerberos and Styx, were found. *New Horizons* captured photos of Charon, Hydra, and Nix.

The photos showed that Charon is just as geologically exciting as Pluto. The large moon has cliffs and canyons covering its surface. One of these canyons may be up to 6 miles (10 km) deep. There are also different bright and dark patches on the moon's surface. These regions may indicate that, like Pluto, Charon's surface has recently changed.

Photos of Hydra revealed that this moon is 27 miles (43 km) long by 20 miles (32 km) wide. Its surface is very reflective. In fact, all four of Pluto's small moons are much brighter than scientists were expecting. This led scientists to believe that the moons are mostly made of water ice. Photos show that Nix has a very large crater.

An artist's impression of what Charon would look like when viewed from the surface of Pluto

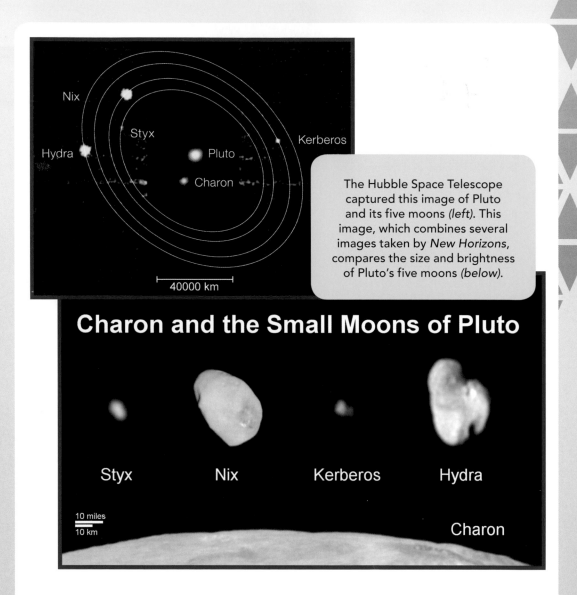

Nix

Styx

Hydra

Pluto

Kerberos

Charon

40000 km

The Hubble Space Telescope captured this image of Pluto and its five moons *(left)*. This image, which combines several images taken by *New Horizons*, compares the size and brightness of Pluto's five moons *(below)*.

Charon and the Small Moons of Pluto

Styx

Nix

Kerberos

Hydra

10 miles
10 km

Charon

Scientists were also surprised about the orbits of the four small moons. None of them have a typical orbit. They wobble and spin. It is difficult to predict which side of each moon might face Pluto every day. These irregular orbits happen because each moon is shaped differently. The moons also orbit both Pluto and Charon, so they are being pulled by the gravity of two large objects instead of just one.

After *New Horizons* zoomed past Pluto and its unpredictable moons, the spacecraft continued on into the Kuiper Belt. *New Horizons* will continue to explore the third zone of the solar system as scientists collect and study the data from Pluto. No matter what *New Horizons* encounters next, its mission succeeded. "With that flyby, *New Horizons* completed a long-held goal of the scientific community and a five-decade-long quest by NASA to explore all the planets known at the start of the space age," Stern said. "And that all got its start 10 years ago with our launch."

WHAT'S NEXT?

As *New Horizons* speeds through the Kuiper Belt, scientists hope that the spacecraft will be able to reach and take close-up photos of a Kuiper Belt object (KBO) known as 2014 MU69. *New Horizons* would reach this object in January 2019. Scientists say that *New Horizons* is in good condition and could last another twenty years. Along with studying 2014 MU69, *New Horizons* would also be able to observe other KBOs and gases in the Kuiper Belt.

Scientists don't just want to continue to explore the Kuiper Belt because it hasn't been done before. They also think that

The Hubble Space Telescope captured this image of KBOs to help the *New Horizons* team decide where to send the spacecraft next.

An artist's image depicts *New Horizons* in the Kuiper Belt *(above)*. An artist's depiction of a KBO *(inset)*

knowing about Pluto and other Kuiper Belt objects will help them understand the history of the solar system and how it was created. KBOs are, in a way, preserved like scientific specimens kept on ice. Pluto and other KBOs contain information about the materials that became planets. Many astronomers believe that KBOs are what's left of the solar system's formation more than four billion years ago. "By looking at these more-primordial bodies, we can better understand the solar system's architecture and formation," said Cathy Olkin, the mission's deputy project scientist.

The *New Horizons* mission is taking space exploration farther into the future of space travel. But it's also revealing plenty about the past.

Source Notes

6 Guy Gugliotta, "NASA Readies to Launch Pluto Mission," *Washington Post*, December 19, 2005, http://www.washingtonpost.com/wp-dyn/content /article/2005/12/18/AR2005121800976.html?sub=AR.

7 Deborah Netburn, "Pluto Is Defying Scientists' Expectations in So Many Ways," *LA Times*, March 17, 2016, http://www.latimes.com/science /sciencenow/la-sci-sn-pluto-landscapes-20160318-story.html.

16 Mike Wall, "Five Years Later, Pluto's Planethood Demotion Still Stirs Controversy," *Space.com*, August 24, 2011, http://www.space.com/12709 -pluto-dwarf-planet-decision-5-years-anniversary-iau.html.

25 "The Women Who Power NASA's New Horizons Mission to Pluto," NASA, last modified July 30, 2015, http://www.nasa.gov/feature/the-women-who -power-nasa-s-new-horizons-mission-to-pluto.

29 Leonard David, "On Pluto Time: Q&A with New Horizons Leader Alan Stern," *Space.com*, October 27, 2015, http://www.space.com/30934-pluto-new -horizons-alan-stern-interview.html.

31 "New Horizons Returns First of the Best Images of Pluto," NASA, December 4, 2015, http://www.nasa.gov/feature/new-horizons-returns-first-of-the-best -images-of-pluto.

33 "The Icy Mountains of Pluto," NASA, July 15, 2015, http://www.nasa.gov /image-feature/the-icy-mountains-of-pluto.

36 Nola Taylor Redd, "Does Pluto Have an Atmosphere?," *Space.com*, February 20, 2016, http://www.space.com/18564-pluto-atmosphere.html.

41 Hub staff, "The Voyage of a Lifetime: Marking a Decade since 'New Horizons' Launch," *Hub*, January 20, 2016, http://hub.jhu.edu/2016/01/20/new-horizons -marks-ten-years-since-launch.

43 Sophie Bushwick, "What We've Learned from the Pluto Flyby," *Popular Science*, November 18, 2015, http://www.popsci.com/exploring-everyones -favorite-former-planet.

Glossary

atmosphere: a mass of gases that surround a planet, star, dwarf planet, or other KBO

computer code: a set of instructions for a computer

crater: a hole created by the impact of a meteor or other debris

demotion: to change the rank or position of something to a lower or less important one

dwarf planet: a round object that orbits the sun like a regular planet but in an orbit that is full of asteroids and other debris. Planets are larger and have a clear path around the sun.

glacier: a large body of ice that moves slowly over an area of land

International Astronomical Union: a group of astronomers who make decisions, such as determining that Pluto is not a planet but a dwarf planet

Kuiper Belt: a ring around the solar system, farther away than Neptune, that is thought to include countless icy objects, such as asteroids, comets, dwarf planets, and other bodies

NASA: National Aeronautics and Space Administration. This US agency oversees the exploration of the stars and planets with manned and unmanned missions.

nitrogen: a chemical that has no color or smell

orbit: the path a spacecraft or other object follows, usually elliptical (egg-shaped), around a planet, moon, or star

plutonium: a radioactive element used to make nuclear energy

space probe: a device used to obtain information from outer space and send it back to Earth

Selected Bibliography

The Discovery of Pluto. Lowell Observatory. Accessed May 16, 2016.
https://lowell.edu/in-depth/pluto/the-discovery-of-pluto/.

Hub staff. "The Voyage of a Lifetime: Marking a Decade since 'New Horizons'
Launch." *Hub*, January 20, 2016. http://hub.jhu.edu/2016/01/20/new
-horizons-marks-ten-years-since-launch.

"New Horizons Marks 10 Years since Launch." NASA, January 19, 2016.
http://www.nasa.gov/feature/new-horizons-marks-10-years-since-launch.

"New Horizons: The First Mission to Pluto and the Kuiper Belt; Exploring
Frontier Worlds." NASA, January 2006. https://www.nasa.gov/pdf
/139889main_PressKit12_05.pdf.

Further Reading

Aguilar, David. *Space Encyclopedia: A Tour of Our Solar System and Beyond.*
Washington, DC: National Geographic, 2013.

Carson, Mary Kay. *Mission to Pluto: The First Visit to an Ice Dwarf and the
Kuiper Belt.* Boston: Houghton Mifflin Harcourt, 2016.

Dunn, Marcia. *New Horizons: Rediscovering Pluto.* Miami: Mango Media /
Associated Press, 2016.

Dwarf Planet Pluto: Facts about the Icy Former Planet
http://www.space.com/43-pluto-the-ninth-planet-that-was-a-dwarf.html

Kops, Deborah. *Exploring Exoplanets.* Minneapolis: Lerner Publications, 2012.

New Horizons
https://www.nasa.gov/mission_pages/newhorizons/main/index.html

Pluto: King of the Kuiper Belt
http://solarsystem.nasa.gov/planets/pluto

Index

Photo Acknowledgments

The images in this book are used with the permission of: NASA/Johns Hopkins University Applied Physics Laboratory/Southwest Research Institute, pp. 2, 4, 7, 13 (bottom), 21, 26 (bottom), 28, 29, 30, 34, 35, 36, 37, 38, 40 (bottom); NASA, pp. 5, 19, 20; NASA/Kim Shiflett, p. 6; © Joe Haythornthwaite/Wikimedia Commons, p. 8; © James Jones/flickr.com (CC BY 2.0), p. 9 (top); © ZUMA Press, Inc/Alamy, p. 9 (bottom); AP Photo, p. 10 (top); © nivium/Wikimedia Commons (CC BY 2.0), p. 10 (bottom); © Lowell Observatory, p. 11; © Galaxy Picture Library/Alamy, p. 12; US Naval Observatory, p. 13 (top); NASA, ESA, and A. Schaller (for STScI), p. 14; ESA/ATG medialab, p. 15 (top); NASA/JPL-Caltech/UCLA/MPS/DLR/IDA, p. 15 (bottom); © Bettina Strenske/Alamy, p. 16; © nagualdesign/Wikimedia Commons (CC0 1.0), p. 17; NASA, ESA, and G. Bacon (STScI), p. 18; Laura Westlund/Independent Picture Service, p. 22; NASA/JHUAPL, p. 23; NASA/New Horizons, p. 24; NASA/Joel Kowsky, p. 25; NASA/JPL, pp. 26 (top), 32, 33; Courtesy LASP, p. 27; NASA/Bill Ingalls, p. 31; ESO/L. Calçada, p. 39; NASA/ESA/L. Frattare (STScI), p. 40 (top); NASA/ESA/SwRI/JHU/APL/New Horizons KBO Search Team, p. 42; © Eugen Dobric/iStock/Thinkstock, p. 43 (top); © Stocktrek Images/Thinkstock, p. 43 (bottom).

Front cover: NASA/Johns Hopkins University Applied Physics Laboratory/Southwest Research Institute.